SHALL WE GO?

Annemarie Austin was born in Devon and grew up on the Somerset Levels and in Weston-super-Mare, where she has lived for most of her life. She won the Cheltenham Literature Festival Poetry Competition in 1980, and her first collection, *The Weather Coming* (1987), was a Poetry Book Society Recommendation. *Very: New & Selected Poems* (Bloodaxe Books, 2008) includes work from her first six collections, including *On the Border* (1993), *The Flaying of Marsyas* (1995), *Door upon Door* (1999) and *Back from the Moon* (2003). She has since published two further collections, *Track* (2014) and *Shall We Go?* (2021).

ANNEMARIE AUSTIN

Shall We Go?

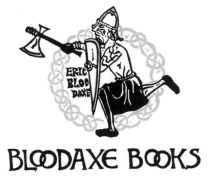

BLOODAXE BOOKS

ISBN: 978 1 78037 553 3

First published 2021 by
Bloodaxe Books Ltd,
Eastburn,
South Park,
Hexham,
Northumberland NE46 1BS.

www.bloodaxebooks.com
For further information about Bloodaxe titles
please visit our website and join our mailing list
or write to the above address for a catalogue

Supported using public funding by

**ARTS COUNCIL
ENGLAND**

Cover design: Neil Astley & Pamela Robertson-Pearce.

Printed in Great Britain by Bell & Bain Limited, Glasgow, Scotland, on
acid-free paper sourced from mills with FSC chain of custody certification.

I sometimes imagine slipping back into an empty theatre at midnight and, in the dark auditorium, catching the scenery refusing to *play the game*...

JULIEN GRACQ

very probably the
world is flatter than one thinks

ROBERT CREELEY

ACKNOWLEDGEMENTS

Acknowledgements are due to the editors of the following publications where some of these poems first appeared: *Ambit*, *Carillon*, *The Interpreter's House*, *Magma*, *New Welsh Review*, *Pennine Platform*, *Poetry London*, *Poetry Wales*, *The Rialto*, *Shearsman* and *Tears in the Fence*.

The epigraphs are from *A Dark Stranger* by Julien Gracq, tr. Christopher Moncrieff (Pushkin Books, 2013) and 'Talking' by Robert Creeley from *On Earth: Last Poems and an Essay* (University of California Press, 2006).

CONTENTS

Shall We Go on the Shiny?

The boy dragged a big spade behind him
across the sand pockmarked by rain
towards where a high tide had left it
smooth and sodden and reflective.
Over his shoulder he asked the woman
'Shall we go on the shiny?'

Not her, she said, but she'd watch
how he grew stiltwalker legs there
like a seagull stretched into heron
and any small ordinary dog which
showed instead as a stately hound
such as posed in swagger portraits.

So he strode out alone with his spade
onto the shiny and so she lost him
digging his way into a dazzle that
raised a wall before her soon enough.
And his footprints were swallowed up
just as fast as he made them.

Nail File

Think of filing down the Atlantic Ocean
which widens every year
at roughly the rate of
a fingernail growing.

There was a rock in that ocean.
There was a bobbing raft.

He stood on the rock and saw
nothing in the water. Nothing
should use that raft
to reach his rock.

So he hauled in the raft by its rope
and tied it to the rock.

After a while he was sure he saw
how this rock diminished as
the Atlantic widened.

And so stood on one leg to be
smaller and more narrow.

He certainly saw how raft and rope
were frayed by the fret of
rock against water.

That was when he thought of
filing down the ocean.

Anything with Beak or Bill

To sup it up, sup it all
up until the lake's a desert
and the little fishes dry
as the remains of dragonflies.

Fruit

I had taken up the cause
of the tiny tan berry
fruited on the air
outside my window,

attending to it each day
from my side of the glass,
though I quickly saw
what it really was –

a snail on a single thread
of spider silk,
fixed by a bubble
of snail spit

or by the spider's artifice.
All the week long
I'd turned to it
where it rocked

on its mooring line
and every morning
let some more
of the daylight through,

its dark small self
inside that spiral
shrinking back and back
very far indeed.

Slow and After

It couldn't get any slower than
this dance of the bronze figure where
one foot is a little ahead in time
of the other foot (weight shifting
only now) and the hip above that
second foot delays its twist until
it knows the shoulder will follow
after and next the extended elbow
and the wrist bringing up the rear
then whatever the other arm is doing
means that it lags and last of all
the fingers of that hand stretch out
in salutation to an answering dip
of the chin and the eyelids lowering

When we came to the Finnish town
the day after the tango festival it
was barely functioning and although
our hotel was open for business
nothing else was (no cafés or shops)
and not even a cat walked deserted
streets that some dust blew across
to pool around the raw wood stages
thrown up wherever spaces were in
emptied car parks and little squares
as dancefloors and more dancefloors
for those partners gazing past each
other towards the midnight forest
and retreat once the morning came

Dances

Pina Bausch said that
when she was dancing with eyes closed
it made a difference where she looked
under her shut lids.
                I thought of this
watching those Christmas trees
dressed in real party clothes –
full skirts and little shiny bodices
pulled over and down their branches –
in the hospice charity shop window.

Above each satin neckline rose
only a small peak of green boughs.
There was looking downwards in the dark
or, to be different, to stare ahead and
butt against the eyelids' linings.

Anything with Paws Before Its Eyes

Because it knows how to shut out light,
how to stifle any shriek arising from
that darkness. Because the world can only
come in at it sideways, pushing like a
sheet of paper against the resolute paws.

Pincer

This cover shielded
a crab's thumb
I've decided – as hard
a lost digit of a glove
as can be imagined
with the sun at work
on its unnecessary glory
of ivory and brick and
black that at sunset
you twist to show
how its knuckle end
is a mihrab shape
is oval over rectangle
prayer slot in the shingle

Form

I had a dress form –
a sort of wire-netting corset
I pressed against my waist and
ribs and breasts, where the hip
swelled and the shoulder knuckled;
then, carefully unbuckled, it served
on its stand for my shed body
(like a crab's?) and did to fit
all bodices against, to pin
and tack them into
submission.

Though I slipped a kind of vest
on it, for best effect, I
remember. Then my pins
had purchase where
otherwise was air
patchworked.

That was Platonic me between
the collar and pubic bones.
Sometimes it shone like
a little silver teapot
or, vest pulled down
on it, resembled
antler velvet.

For form was fiercer than shape
would be – that could lie on a
party plate impersonating
rabbit in blancmange.

This was birdcage on
a pole, this was pot
to catch the crab
to be cut up.

Problem

...the insurmountable difficulties presented by certain philosophic problems arise from the fact that we separate out in space, phenomena which do not occupy space.

HENRI BERGSON

She's not the one but
they have to put her somewhere

somewhere she can't
bump up against the rest whoever

they might be. What clarifies is
the space around each figure

the haloing of the hermit
in his cave in the desert.

Put her in the desert perhaps
but keep her away from

other hermits. Imagine
the consequence of their breath

entwining across the cave
the haloes interlocking.

There mustn't be merging
smudge is forbidden

they say or don't say but
act on in her case.

*

Examine her without a background
ignore the negative space

bore in on her concentrating
look and look and look until

she's seen right through and out
the other side on which there's

nothing to do but return
come the opposite way

arrive in front of her who's become
a structure of tunnels a sort of

perforated alp of a person though
the grid of her's not fine

enough yet and she must be
pierced and pierced at another point

another point. Undo this woman
who just stands there who just

looks back at them because
her eyes have been rendered routes

her arm and leg bones pathways
and they come and go through her

so fast they miss where they've been
have to reiterate that passage

unsupplied with resting places
nowhere to stop and know her.

It's relentless to and fro and dig
another tunnel. She stands there.

*

Inside the woman her memory
of the undoing spider

the one that had second thoughts
and let the bee go although

she had bound it already
into a white buzzing tube.

The woman had seen that.
Then the woman had heard

the bee's buzz grow louder
so she looked again

and the tube had put out a leg
then another there was a wing

and the spider busy at its
unwinding motion to one side.

She remembered a moment of
consideration on both parts

the spider of its work before
returning to a corner

the bee of its constriction gone
away and sudden freedom

it resolved to use in a scoop
of flight down and off.

*

The house enters
house-arrested her

its balcony her shoulders
her ribs the balustrade

should she lie on her side
considering a garden.

The grain of the floorboard
is growing through her cheek

her ear its imitation. She can hear
the knives in the drawer

the door remaining closed. Her mouth
is open as the window in the

gable end mortared with all
her hair stirred into the mixture.

Polly Vaughan – Variations

1

Have I mistaken you, my swan,
dipping your head, dipping your neck
among the leaves' undershadows
over the black water?
                    Are you a girl
who's wrapped her apron round her,
wrapped her head and her neck and
shoulders in white laundry? Are you
maybe the Polly Vaughan I love?

Polly Vaughan rhymes with swan
and covered head rhymes with dead.
And when dusk rises from the water
it's hard to tell bird from woman
in the leaves and leaves and shadow.

2

Didn't she play
the part of swan –
crouched in the bushes
cloaked in white?

The girl from her covert
watched the hunters
as a bird does
still as a bowstring
not yet touched.

She wanted to be unseen
and no one saw her
for herself but as

25

a great pale swan
beside the water.

So Polly Vaughan is dead
tangled in her torn apron
like disordered plumage
reddened with bird blood.

3

They are wrong when they say
she'd wound herself with her linen
so appeared a fowl to be shot

Some women like Polly Vaughan
transform at night to creatures

Customarily when darkness fell
she was swan on the black pond

Come by stealth to this retreat
then like Actaeon barging in
he it was turned her back into
that jumble of cloth and woman

The Unidentified

Who's been obliterated here, she asks,
staring at the white board on legs
that tells her just three things:

which plot the unidentified was
buried in, then date and location
of that whoever's annihilation

in the blanket bombing her parents
chanced to have been in the town for.
She recalls snatches of their stories:

her mother in the black street in her
nightgown, how what seemed fast
annoying insects were bullets;

most of all, her serviceman father's
assignment to gather body fragments
from the beach into a wheelbarrow.

(I had shaken and shaken
the earth from my roots until
they were white string for
the brown-paper parcel of myself
knots bloody with sealing wax)

Identify – 'to determine the identity of';
then, looking in the dictionary
for the origins of 'identity':

idem   to be the same
entitas   entity
identidem over and over.

There's an entity in the grave,
the earth pulled round it,
but no one who met that before
has recognised such repetition
and called out a name, an age,
history or gender to give it again.

(I should meditate upon
the character of chasms
how they maintain themselves
with little alteration
through geological time
being more emptiness
than substance
and the emptiness defining)

Let me phrase the question
in a different way, she says.

What god dropped this body
no longer needed as disguise?

What god then reared up in all
its unbearable incendiary nature,

taking the eyes and gesturing flesh
of lookers-on to be one with its burning?

Razzle-dazzle

Stars in the night
Blazing their light
Can't hold a candle –
To your razzle-dazzle.

YIP HARBURG

It was Mary Zekiel explained
how an angel had parked its wings
there on the coat-and-hat stand
just inside the front door in the dim.
She was presumed to know about such things.

But I always thought of you not-quite-dressed,
                              anyway,
taking out the pins.

                    (Queen Elizabeth's costumes
were built of independent segments from
separate chests – undersleeves, oversleeves,
three-part skirts and bodice fronts – anchored
for the moment by bright pins that clicked
and pinged to the floors as she went away.)

...when they stood, they let down their wings.

If any of us tried to fly by sewing
pillows to armholes and making
makeshift wings, they'd be in trouble,
Mary Zekiel reminded. Such things
were always professional undertakings.

But I thought of you sloughing off your sleeves,
                              anyway,
undoing fastenings.

29

(On Queen Elizabeth's
dresses jewels were transferred from bodice
to bodice as required, knots of pearls unknotted
to star in those portraits sent to the ends of
the kingdom in her stead, to embody her self –
so suffer embedding in poison or stabbing
with hog bristles, burning. Men died for such acts.)

And he put forth the form of an hand, and took me by
a lock of mine head.

Oh look at you without your wings. What a
pretty thing.
           What a smooth and luminous figure
at the end of the passage going away.
                        Today
Mary Zekiel didn't need to make me aware of
your arrival.
           For you flared and dazzled where
the shadows should have been deepest.
                      There are
dark shapes of you left behind in my eyes.

Botafumeiro

The incense bottle flew above us and
I felt a galloping within. The wind of it
blew a hole in me resonant as a bell.

Now I'm used to that opening, though
I sobbed at the base of a pillar then
when the great swinging was done with.

It galloped off like those horses dragging
the runaway coach I rode in in my dream,
the steppe to either side of me like wings.

Or it flew away farther than the total
transept width and out of the huge rose
windows (are they those windows? – never mind).

A hole remained. Because I was there,
strange certainty in the air above me pulling
a trail of smoke behind it across the aisles

and back again, swinging out on a lengthening
rope until it hung horizontal and impossible,
still for a long count, a breath. My breath

shifted away from me, to be on its own on
the incense bottle's track. Those echoes in
my head spoke the round empty left behind.

I'm not converted but thrown down nonetheless
by the passage of something much more than
itself that descended then, that escaped again.

Santiago de Compostella

Camino

Pilgrims would record the stations of their pilgrimage on large sheets
of thick paper they then used to cover themselves at night.

I begin this corner of my counterpane:

We stopped for the porch of forgiveness
at Carrión de los Condes, though only one
among us was to renounce his pilgrimage
(the sore on his leg become too much to bear).
The little yard around the church's end was
thick with bright-green four-leafed clovers.

On the road surface someone had painted
'baccanal', and a pole propped against a wall
had a chicken head and yellow chicken feet
below its sprigged-winceyette night clothes.
A passing group of youths sported pillow slips
with black-edged cut-outs for eyes.

That made me tired. It made me think of
the counterpane, to cover pillowcases and
those childish nightgowns the animals wore.

True Vessel

He reached deep into the sequinned bag –
it was the size and shape of the calico one
they'd made me write my name on in the dream –
and said 'I like gifts which don't last.' I didn't
know my real name in that dream but was told
it was 'Vera Flagon'. True vessel, I thought,
I like that. 'I like to put in a lot of effort and
have nothing to show for it at the end,' the boy
listed next – by then I had pen and paper out
and under the café table was writing down
what he said. The sequins shifted and glinted.
My dreamt cotton bag had been much plainer
even when labelled 'Vera Flagon' in huge blue
felt-pen letters I translated as true vessel.
'I like people to steal things when they come
to my house,' he finally declared – I found that
much later where I'd put it away in the bag.

Which Conceals the Location of Waterholes

In the fold between the pages,
in the place where you wait
before it happens, the space
in the dresser that isn't plates,
the lobby, the vestibule, the void
under the table.

        For breathing,
for a little verdigris to settle
on the skin, for the building or
destruction of dust castles, for
folding hands.

        And watching light
track across the white wall
between pictures and dive into
their glass, wring itself out,
hang on a line to dry and flap
and twist away.

        Into shadow at
the corner, into the gutter of
the book, the unlit anteroom
with random chairs and deeper
darkness that sits exact
under each of them in the gloom.

Hole

A hole is defined
solely by what it's not.
The cave is a kind of
out of.
      But no one
would have come
for just the cliff.

Between the Yews

What are ways may
also be caskets what
are caskets borders that
liquefy like *Orphée*'s
mirror through to a way
down inside its treasure
chest though windowed
like the enclosed stair
up to the Serbian church
at Eger or this yew-locked
route with alternating
shadows thrown onto
the bright-mossed path
where from the dream
remembered De Chirico's
long-haired girl bowls
her hoop down the slope
in front of me between
the goblet-cut yews
cutting out all beyond
so the way is box indeed
is precious illuminated
casket waiting for me
to take a step that is
to push back the lid that
is to open up this quite
other place than the grey
surrounding graveyard

Marquise

The marquise went out at five o'clock
        under a cloud

The marquise went out at five o'clock
        counting it up
        on the fingers of one hand

The marquise went out at five o'clock
        in a hat of
        astonishing feathers
        but gloves with
        a split seam

The marquise went out at five o'clock
        having eaten
        a macaroon
        in preparation

The marquise went out at five o'clock
        when nobody should
        know or notice

The marquise went out at five o'clock
        despite the distance

The marquise went out at five o'clock
        over the stone bridge
        and past
        the sickly potted palms

The marquise went out at five o'clock
        as if she were skating
        down a tunnel

The marquise went out at five o'clock
        with a little knife
        in her sleeve

The marquise went out at five o'clock
        to where
        the shadow
        was deepest
        under the trees

In the *Surrealist Manifesto* André Breton quoted Paul Valéry's dislike of such sentences as 'The marquise went out at five o'clock'. Roland Barthes made use of it to deplore the limitations of the simple past tense.

The Unspoken

It's not as if it pushed up inside
against the teeth, not as if the teeth
constrained it behind a white paling
fence or a line of upright stones
so it had to lean there mourning,
not as though it cried out silently
lying on the soft bed of the tongue
distraught. If it was anguished
that was not apparent in the dark
mouth cave whose paintings no one
had yet brought torches to, nobody
came to investigate their waiting
symbols. The tongue might feel for
the hole in a tooth but never touch
its root where perhaps the unspoken
brooded, packed into viscera and
within blood vessels in the deepest
back yard among other terracotta
pots. I thought how new compost
stains the concrete after heavy rain,
though weight could not squeeze
one syllable from this gristle.

Latent Levitation

Lying in wait,
that rising by reason of lightness.
It can be, but probably not today
when my wrists weigh heavy.

Look at Goya's old women ascending
with tambourines, the one with a guitar
who hovers above her fellow, singing.
Their faces are delighted. Of course,

of course. I should remember
that I can do this (the skimming
dreams when only a hop of the will
was needed to keep me airborne).

Even that hermit woman,
offended at her funeral by the crowd's
massed stink, could rise
into the roof until the aisles were clear

as if she were a lit paper lantern.
What's the trick? It's the very
release of that weight on my wrists
that will set me flying.

Line Drawing

Drew the line and let it go
free
     maybe taken by balloon
on a wind from the sea

Space grew where the line
had been
        Hard not to fill it
with more pencil
            Drew the line
and crossed it with another
watched them take off in
opposite directions
           leaving
a rose-knot of air behind

Wove a net of lines
          to catch
the air
     that slithered through
Drew a circle
       made a noose
pulled it in and in
         on nothing
Drew the line and let it go

Tightrope

'Love destroys the centre of gravity
in tightrope dancers' – and so we must
keep them enclosed and nunlike.

In the afternoons they do painting-by-
numbers or colour-in their colouring
books. Nuns don't, but the analogy

still seems valid when they walk
the line like some cloister path
narrowed down and lit bizarrely

(Darling!), or repetitions on the training
treadmill serve as those rosary beads
between the fingers and Hail Marys

on the lips. (Practised kissing the back
of my hand or leaving a rosebud
print on a mirror for a moment.)

It's only minutes in the spotlight
upright on the apparent air we ask
of them, the habits of nuns flung down

into the darkness. Dressed now in scales
and feathers who shall separate them
from the love of God? They play as

birds or insects between the unseen
earth and presumed sky. (From very high,
picked out a suitor in the crowd.)

The Walking Shot

Once you have found
the man to follow,
come up behind him
till a yard or so still
separates you. Wait
for his setting off then
set off too. One, two,
coordinate your pace
with his, tread where
he treads. Follow that
intractable slab of
his back, not expecting
to see woods except
peripherally. Don't
plan to overtake him
or to stretch the gap
between you. You've
bought into this walking
shot and its narrow
plod continues. Marriage
is like this in his world,
the desert coming up
to right and left of you.

The Misses Booth Photographed by Camile Silvy

1

This parting in my hair is more meticulous than
seems possible. I balance one side of a mirror upon it.

I could draw a diagram of this pose,
its placing on the ground, then the glass behind,
another picture plane but willing itself forward.

I can feel that intention press against my shoulder,
sense the mirror tipping its liquid darkness out.
My back is drenched by spill I cannot see.

I am sick of looking nowhere a long time
when dark is seeping between my neck and earring.

2

My parting is more meticulous than seems possible.
I balance the other side of the mirror upon it.

I have hidden my hands. I have turned away.
Admire my back hair uplifted in pinned coils.
That's almost all I'm giving you, the rest
filled with the enormous plainness of my crinoline.

You'll find my voice difficult to hear
among material folds and doubled hems,
that swag of curtain velvet behind my sister.
And the hard mirror surface setting up echoes.

3

'I conjure you,' he said.

I hover a little back from the back of the looking-glass.
It does for a doorway when I am in the corridor behind.
My parting is a faint blurred line.

They have crossed their upstage arms against me,
the littlest one. I shall not look at them,
in my own place like a casket, with mother-of-pearl.

How sweet the darkness on my cheek.
I think it must be a velvet pillow
and I its conjured jewel.

The Tour

The only dusty photograph was
her mother's. Her lover's showed
the back of his head as he turned
to her flattering smiling image.

Oh I don't like you, I thought.
Which wouldn't have perturbed her.

The portrait of her father was
far larger than the others and
angled towards the bed – where
she could see it from her pillow.

This matched how her conversation
so often turned in his direction.

Dead, dead, alive but absent,
they were. My mother made me
nothing when she reached out to
the bread on the table behind me

knowing her hand would pass through
my transparency, my dissolution.

And she is dead. I gave all her
photographs to my sister who has
children and can pass them on.
I turned away from children.

In Sight

I heard her shout 'Don't
turn your back on the sea!'
to a child in the shallows,
but I didn't see her face or
what she feared, the waves
behaving much as usual.

The sparrows in the hedge
never want you watching.
When I draw abreast of where
they are – little plump drab
bodies in the lattices of twigs –
they fall silent, freeze...
don't rebegin their racket
until I'm three steps past.

And the sea when my back's
to it articulates completely the
pulse and pressure and commotion
of its action I can't retain
when eyes are also taking in
the glitter off the wave crests
breaking in the peopled sea
under a pale inflated sky.

Maybe Oystercatchers

When you give a child the name of a bird – it loses the bird.

JOYCE CARY

What I had was
the slim black slants of them,
their size (smaller than the same-
angle crows, which were
thicker as if ballasted below
about the stomach).

They were out near the edge
of the tide and silhouetted and
I wondered were they oystercatchers
and if they were what was the gain
in adding red legs I could not see
to the profiled slants I did.

Then I passed a couple
who laughed at their child for
calling the pigeons 'chickens' (though
those scattered before her tottering
run just as chicken would,
staying on the ground).

So I had my doubts looking out
from the train to London
at the Uffington white horse
no longer a thing of lines
having gained a bellyful
of snow below its slanting spine.

Waterscape

Waterscape and the horse stepping through
on its coffin bones makes waves
likely to reach you later
unintelligibly

Wake can take a while to break on
the far shore Near Skokloster
how I puzzled at the sudden
agitation by my feet

Phalanges in lake water like the horse's
and my toe-end nail bones
the same as the coffins
of its hooves

though I cannot wade *en pointe* as it does
making the shallows eddy and
peak up at a distance
against your shoes

Wishes for the Poem as Object

You could make a paper boat
of this poem, if it weren't
a paper boat already.

You could shape an aeroplane
to fly across the room – look
though, it's flying now.

I'll let you turn down the page
and crease it as a dog ear
to start the barking.

You can mark the words and lines
in ink or score a stanza
with your thumbnail –

but the poem's underpainting will
show its skulls or planets
through any overwriting

and be hung up there on the wall
in the good natural light
from a great window.

You can throw it down
but it will crawl away. You
can carry it to another

country and leave it at the station
to catch the train it fancies
all by itself.

When the poem's trapped in a burning
building, it will remember
how to float and fly.

Table/Field

How round this anecdote is.
How it's heen rubbed down
until it fits the hand, fits
the lips again, can be held
in the cheek like a sweet.

(Though the boiled sweet held
too long wears the slick off
the skin of the inside cheek.)

It's currency here. We're old
and our anecdotes roll about
the table. I'm tired of this
but powerless to interrupt
the ritual game of billiards.

(The metaphors get away
to lodge in the green-baize
pockets just as in a mouth.)

Imagine a plain field where
you've been lying. You sit up
to see the pleasing levelness
and the gates in four hedges
that offer a choice of routes.

(We could be old that way.
We could choose an appealing gate
and open it and go through.)

Godney

But if I go to it through the new
still-unpainted gate, will I find
the little sister as a half-known thing
like a snail unbelievable in its shell?

Will I hold in my hand the just-skinned
rabbit tails and carry them in my pocket
for their softness one by one everywhere?

And that cockatoo, its crest the only
colour in the whitewashed empty room.
Will it stay for me there? Will I hear
those withies growing all night long?

Kids Don't Take Walks

'Kids don't take walks,' he says. 'They don't sunbathe
or sit on the porch.'

DON DeLILLO

'Kids don't take walks' but,
like this child in pink, may run
between two invisible points
and when each one is reached,
stand there with legs akimbo
and outstretched arms to a count
of four before setting off again.

In that book I found a picture
of the place that was home until
I was five. Half wild and half
just unkempt at winter's end,
with dead-grass mats, bare
willow branches, full-up rhynes
to follow to left or right if
there were somewhere for a foot.
But the ditches close together
at the photo's edge and then
go on below the frame. Anyone
would have to walk on water.

What did I do as a kid there?
Decades on, there's little I've
retained. 'I took my mirror
into the garden, and the grass
looked in it!' my small niece
told me with great indignation.
The unmoving risen winter ditches
make mirrors of everywhere,

the grass overlapping looking in,
the black branches looking in.
And I look in quite unreflected,
though surely this mirror's mine.

I Go on It and

It's territory.
This is my beach because I go on it
and go on it. If I were a tom cat
I'd mark it with piss-spray.
But anyway, I recognise
my footprints when I'm coming
back on them.

Here the dog knocked me down
that launched itself with all
four feet against my side
having arrived full tilt
from very far away.
Its gap-toothed Irish owner said
'He must know you.'

Well, both of us knew the territory,
both felt it belonged to us.
I left my print on the half-dry sand
that left its print on my jacket
all the way home.
You could see where the dog
had taken flight from the ground.

Sometimes I expect to be caught by
kite strings as a fly by the spider's
filaments. Or fishing lines stretched
too far back to their owners' rods
from the still-distant tide
that catch the light
just in time.

His father kept trying to catch his eye, but the small boy in the white cap was having none of it, being all in all intent on standing in the shallows of the sea with his legs apart, as if keeping a balance were not yet something he could take for granted. The water barely licked his ankles. He stared inland.

Whenever his father tried for his attention, the child changed direction so no one was in his sight. He stared inland.

Until at last that contemplation turned to action, and he dipped his left hand in the tide, drew it out and shook it hard. Four or five or six times he kicked back the little arriving waves. Then lifted his right arm to point the way those waves were going, before stepping off ahead of them inland.

And I've seen a grown man
beckon the sea in with both arms
as he sat on a sand pile.
The territory can be reconfigured easily.
The kneeling girl sinks her fingers
into it and lifts them,
her palms pat it down.

When the beach in drizzle is
all standing water and
there's only me and a few wet gulls,
I hear their fast slopping flurries
like the slap of paddles shaping butter –
first one then another mashing
with webbed feet a hole to peck about in.

There was the baby did much the same.
Rain arrived across the bare mud
with a distinct hiss.
A child half into a mackintosh,
her toes in an overflow runnel
on the slope, said small and hopefully
'Maybe the rain will make some sea.'

It made trenches,
dug channels to redirect the waves
and moats if you like
to ruinous dissolving sandcastles.
It stood in the letters of the messages
traced with stick or spade
for the tide to read then erase.

It was midday, the sun December low. A cloud of oystercatchers
along the receding edge of the sea had three aspects: assemblage
of arrowing black shapes flying in unison; almost nothing at all
when they banked and shifted sideways; and astonishing white
bright glitteriness, almost globular, like ball bearings tossed into
the light. When they disposed themselves along the water's edge,
it was those ball bearings trickled fast from a hand. A bouncing,
exhilarating delight – though sometimes it was cruciform black
arrows instead, sometimes a vanishing slide to the side, the slide
sideways back into sight but shifted, shifting perhaps to the silver-
white balls that were tossed then trickled from a hand.

With the sight of a crow or jackdaw
on the territory
comes the thought of how to draw it.
Since it's black, dense
and almost a flat shape,
I decide on compressed charcoal
with detail of the edges worked in ink.

There's otherwise little more
for the pencil than a line of shore,
some clouds and rubbed-out gulls.
And a stoppered empty plastic squash bottle
bowling and bowling fast over the sand
in a long tumbling slant
spooked all the birds.

Until it stalled in the gulley
of a freshwater outflow.
There's always something plastic to be seen.
Like the blue crate with stuck-on
'Shakespeare' labels the fisherman
must have borrowed from a classroom
to set up on the beach next to his rod.

It said Proper Job
on the yellow carrier bag of the narrow man
who very slowly followed the highwater mark
with his black dog. He was collecting
tiny lumps of sea-washed coal,
mostly no bigger than a thumbnail.
And avoided my eyes.

When I turned to walk north on the beach, there was a group of
four under the pier and one of them set off along the edge of the
sea towards me, scattering pale ash from a plastic bag with the
action of a sower. Because the tide was ebbing, that ash settled
mostly on wet sand in long swathes the westerly wind tugged
inland. I stopped my walk, unwilling to have someone's dust in my
clothes or my hair, between my teeth, but the sower came nearer
and nearer and ash streamed as far up the beach as it was possible
to go. Then just in time the man halted, saying something inaudible,
the plastic bag with a hole in its corner suddenly empty.

The group under the pier waited matter-of-factly. One picked
up and examined a fragment of the ash near his feet. So I resumed
my progress, stepping over the grey swathes, until I reached those
three. Then we went in opposite directions.

You see I go on it continually,
that territory that has
no end in terms of duration.

At its base and its heart is flux
whatever events occur
and who has there
their entrances and exits.

Far enough off on the shore
a bald-headed man who walks away
is confusable with
a naked-faced man walking towards you.
And when you can't decide
which of the few sets
of footprints is his,

the possibility that he might
have been walking backwards
enters the mix. Sand shrimps
in holes dug by my heels
at the edge of the tide,
whirl round and round like
tiny bleached Catherine wheels.

Ostensibly the beach was very smooth
on that occasion. But close up
it showed as all over webbed with
narrow wandering incised tracks as
a salt marsh is webbed with creeks.
And it glittered as if
the broken pale shells were mica.

Grey Area

At the corner of the eye a slink,
a quiver, shudder, too fast a speed
or very slow alteration;

maybe the not-grandmother again
making that cushion sink down
in the empty basket chair's

grey area. 'Nobody sees you when
you're old,' she said, but wicker
creaks in the way of her

sitting down. A settling like churned
clay in water or dust motes
coming to rest on shine

is all that's caught by a turned
head. 'When you are old and not
a grandmother, what are you?'

she used to ask. That grey area
stirs uneasily. They'd laugh it off
instead of giving answer.

Like My Pocket

...a naked icon without a frame (like my pocket)...

KASIMIR MALEVICH

Like my pocket
the dimensions
of a space
I can properly look at

And perhaps
the dimensions of
that space I
look out from

The naked icon
streams in my head
from corner
to corner

not a seen thing
and yet not
something unseen
for here it is

behind my eyes
its background
gold breathing
in the light

Less light
in my pocket
more a half gloom
I have to

feel a way through
as to a seat
when the film's
already started

and streams off
from side to side
top to hottom
like the naked icon

to touch
to kiss
though the moving
picture refuses

No frame
to pin it down
like my pocket
that always has

a space
to go in and
out of and
in again

Cut Out

The ins and outs of this
corrugated cardboard make me
remember that queen's tomb
too high to show her face to
commoners (that was for God
looking down) but offering instead
the view of a round jewel-crusted
hem with little unworn shoe soles
at its centre and the stone petticoat
edges winding in and out and
crowding with convolution
that space between

Though in this case such
twining must hide away
inside the cardboard cut-out
figure of an unknown someone
(mostly outline against the light)
who's set up here to be seen by
each passer-by as absolute shallow

But I'm thinking of the pleating
of air and darkness at the back of
that vivid laminated surface
its complication of channels and
shafts like woodwind reeds
as flexible as leaves are
for rolling and folding and pressing
into the depth expressed through
layers of petticoats crowding

Nijinsky Jumps

Between two sources of light
and an interior wall of his asylum
Nijinsky jumps into the air because
a photographer asked him.
                              Or someone
asked. His half-seen face is obedient
but not emotionally involved. 'I can
do this' it says, his feet in that old
first position, his arms in flight –
for one hand is a blur like a bird
up too quick for the shutter speed.

The other hand is lost in his double
shadow.

        (And shadow almost always
complicates a story – some little dark
midday plinth become a long and
gesturing figure like a frantic tree
after teatime.
                      In one antique image
of a Chinese execution, that shadow
stays an intact crosslegged man
though his severed head is flying
through the air.)

                      Nijinsky's suit jacket
has filled with air that presses at
the buttons to give him a sudden belly.
Its padded shoulders have lifted ahead
of his own, and the back of the collar is
a peak his shadow dangles from.

(This in one bigger greyer element of
the double thing two light sources
out of sight are making of his jump.
And shadow as usual complicates
the story, where over the dangled
grey a darker sharper shape's
become three-quarters of a crucifix.)

He has jumped high. He hangs now
in a lonely place against the almost
anonymous wall, his round head lit.
That eleventh-century Carrizo Christ
shows the same walrus-ivory pallor
and identical wide-awake eyes with
pits for pupils. Nijinsky's fifty-one.

It (After Linnaeus)

The double does it all.
Sweeps up and dusts.
Over the rim of the cup
I see her lean to it.

I am idle while this
goes on in a swirl of
skirt and elbows and
implements clashing.

When only one I had to
do it on my own. But
with the double came
leisure for observation.

As Linnaeus, at the door
to deliver his lecture,
found himself already
present and at work.

And turned, went away,
leaving his double to
it. Here she is ready
to compose this poem.

Lop-sided

If you are right-handed
you take your quill
from the left wing
of a goose or swan.

But what if it was the nuns
who made me this way
insisting insisting
that I stop stop
picking up the chalk
with thumb and fingers
on the Devil's side?

I arrange my long hair
poking in pins from the left.
I hold babies (they tell me)
the wrong way round –
their weight on my right elbow
so the left hand's free.

Left-handed is kinder to swans
whose living wings
must be plucked for quills...
With every writer on Heaven's side
each goose in the vicinity
leans in that same direction.

Bringing in the Washing

To set off in that direction
struck by lightning
while bringing in the washing
for his sister

was not what he had meant
boarding a boat to cross
an ocean tasting
the wind's origin shift

Nor she
not on that ladder coming
down the fire escape
a child watched

who took the drill for real
and saw
her hair burn redder going
against descent

Where plumbline meets
clothesline
is marked by
such a fingerpost as

at the corner of the park
with one of
its pointers lettered
NOT HERE

helps nobody
buried at the crossroads
who never knows
which way to go away

The Place of Stations

*...before the railways were built, what took
the place of stations in our dreams?*

The way to go away
has all sorts of wriggles in it –
of the too-broad shoulders
through the transom window
on that back door

or shoulders again, shaking off
a hand that would detain
them, and the toss of the head
demonstrating I don't care.

God had begun to do it
in the fresco in Rome's San Clemente,
his lower arm extruding
from the rainbow-edged disc of heaven,
the sleeve of a white robe
tossed back from his hand.

And it might have been such an escape
when monks of Maiden Bradley
laid hold on God a second, to be left
as he wriggled away
with the part of his coat they claimed
to possess in their clutches.

Those interfaces did to take the place
of stations. Dreamt pieces
of God went in and out of them
leaving brief traces.

Meanwhile when jumper fibres
remain for clues
on the frame of a transom window
I don't care,
being altogether gone this time.